>CONTRIBUTORS

ULI Senior Executives

Patrick L. Phillips
Global Chief Executive Officer, ULI; President,
ULI Foundation

Cheryl Cummins
Executive Officer

Michael Terseck
Chief Financial Officer/Chief Administrative Officer

Lela Agnew
Executive Vice President, Strategic Communications

Kathleen B. Carey
Chief Content Officer

Lisette van Doorn
Chief Executive Officer, ULI Europe

John Fitzgerald
Chief Executive Officer, ULI Asia

David Howard
Executive Vice President, Development and
ULI Foundation

Jason Ray
Chief Technology Officer

Marilee Utter
Executive Vice President, District Councils

ULI Project Staff

Kathleen Carey
Chief Content Officer

Stockton Williams
Executive Director
ULI Terwilliger Center for Housing

Rachel MacCleery
Senior Vice President, Content
ULI Building Healthy Places Initiative

Michelle McDonough Winters
Senior Visiting Fellow
ULI Terwilliger Center for Housing

Camille Galdes
Senior Research Associate, Content

Maya Brennan
Vice President for Housing
ULI Terwilliger Center for Housing

James A. Mulligan
Senior Editor

David James Rose
Manuscript Editor/Managing Editor

Betsy Van Buskirk
Creative Director

Arc Group Ltd.
Graphic Design

Craig Chapman
Senior Director, Publishing Operations

Belden Russonello Strategists LLC

Nancy Belden
Partner

John Russonello
Partner

Christina Lien
Consulting Senior Analyst

> COVER LETTER

This second edition of the biennial Urban Land Institute community survey, *America in 2015* takes the pulse of our country. ULI conducts the survey to illuminate a core question for every American: what do we want in our communities?

America in 2015 describes a nation where generally high levels of overall satisfaction partially mask differences in preferences and perceptions depending on demographic cohort, economic standing, community characteristics, and racial/ethnic background.

Satisfaction. Although most Americans express satisfaction with the communities and places they call home, there are some pockets of discontent worth paying attention to. When it comes to community quality of life, low-income people and renters are less satisfied than others. Millennials and renters—the most likely to be moving—are also the least satisfied with the housing options they have to choose from in their communities. At the other end of the age spectrum, the oldest Americans are the least confident that they will be able to afford the home they want in the future.

Health. Americans across the board express strong sentiment about living in communities where they can be healthy. A clean environment and convenient access to fresh food are top priorities. Yet many communities are not meeting those desires, and a striking number of Americans report living in places where it is unsafe to walk outside, where fresh food is not available, and where other barriers to healthy lifestyles exist. It seems that many places are missing a major opportunity to retain and attract residents, and the survey provides strong evidence that community design is contributing to troubling health trends. The findings also suggest strong opportunities for new retail and services.

Preferences. Nearly half of Americans, and three-fourths of millennials, say they plan to move in the next five years. Due to the size of this generational cohort, millennials represent a demographic juggernaut. Many millennials prefer walkable, bikable communities, and 63 percent would like to live where they do not need a car often; they also prefer culturally diverse communities. While a plurality of millennials would live in cities if they could live anywhere, a majority say they want single-family homes and believe they will be able to achieve that goal. Millennials represent a strong driver of demand for compact, mixed-use development formats, in suburban or other locations.

The findings from *America in 2015* have profound implications for the nation's leaders in the responsible use of land. As the economy continues its recovery and the country's demographic transformation continues, ULI will remain deeply engaged in assessing the data, identifying the trends, and elevating the best practices for creating the communities that Americans call home.

We hope you enjoy the report. We invite you to explore the findings in more detail at www.uli.org/communitysurvey.

Rachel MacCleery
Senior Vice President, Content
ULI Building Healthy Places Initiative

Stockton Williams
Executive Director
ULI Terwilliger Center for Housing

$\rangle$ CONTENTS

EXECUTIVE SUMMARY   2

HOW WE FEEL
Satisfaction with Communities and Housing   8

WHAT WE VALUE
Community Attribute Priorities   12

BARRIERS TO HEALTHY LIVING
Community Design and Health   16

WHAT WE WANT
Car Use, Diversity, and Location   22

WHERE WE LIVE
Housing Choices and Outlook   26

ABOUT THE SURVEY   31

> EXECUTIVE SUMMARY

In 2013, ULI published a national survey of Americans' preferences and priorities regarding their communities, housing, and transportation. *America in 2013* found that Americans were mostly satisfied with the quality of life in their communities and uncovered a strong desire for compact and mixed-use communities. *America in 2015* expands upon the 2013 survey approach with new questions exploring priorities for and barriers around healthy communities and lifestyles. With a sample of 1,201 respondents, the survey's national findings have a 2.9 percent margin of error.

HOW WE FEEL
Satisfaction with Communities and Housing

Americans overall express high levels of satisfaction with their communities and the homes in which they live. These expressions of satisfaction are very high for all demographic groups, although they dip among certain groups such as those with lower incomes, millennials, and renters.

- Eighty-seven percent of Americans are somewhat or very satisfied with the quality of life in their community, 88 percent are satisfied with their current homes, and 81 percent are satisfied with the housing options in their communities.

- Renters are less satisfied with their homes and communities than owners, and a quarter of renters are dissatisfied with their housing options.

- Millennials are the least-satisfied age group: 15 percent are dissatisfied with their community's quality of life and their current homes, and 21 percent are dissatisfied with their housing options.

50%
of people say walkability is a top or high priority when considering where to live.

Generations

18–36

Millennials, ages 18 to 36 (also known as generation Y), are the most diverse generation and most likely to live in cities, and also the most likely to be expecting to move in the next five years.

37–49

Generation Xers, ages 37 to 49, are predominantly owners of single-family homes and are the least likely to desire urban amenities, and many are expecting to move to larger quarters within five years.

25% OF RENTERS ARE DISSATISFIED WITH THE RANGE OF HOUSING OPTIONS IN THEIR COMMUNITY.

50–68

Baby boomers, ages 50 to 68, are the most likely to live in the suburbs, and unlike generation X they are more likely to be moving to smaller homes than larger ones in the next five years.

69+

The silent generation and the war babies are combined in this report. The war babies (ages 69 through 84) and the silent generation (ages 85 and older) are most likely to already live in rural areas and small towns. If they move, it will be to a more convenient and accessible area.

ACCESS TO FRESH, HEALTHY FOOD IS A TOP OR HIGH PRIORITY FOR **73%** OF THE COUNTRY.

WHAT WE VALUE
Community Attribute Priorities

Survey respondents were asked about their priorities when it comes to what they want from where they live. A healthy environment rises to the top of the priority list, with healthy air and water and access to fresh, healthy food leading the pack.

- When considering where to live, the vast majority of people (87 percent) say that the quality of the environment is a top or high priority.

- How walkable a neighborhood is—including sidewalks, pedestrian crosswalks, and so forth—is a top or high priority for half of the public.

- A third (32 percent) say that having public transit is a high or top priority, with more low-income people sharing this view.

BARRIERS TO HEALTHY LIVING
Community Design and Health

Despite the high priority placed on healthy community elements, a significant number of Americans face community design–related barriers to living a healthy lifestyle. While most people say they can easily access fresh food, African Americans and Latinos report greater difficulty. A considerable share of the population also says their community lacks

Low-Income Americans

For the purposes of this report, low-income Americans are defined as those earning at or below 200 percent of the federal poverty level for 2014. This income level varies by household size from $24,000 for an individual to $47,700 for a family of four. Low-income Americans represent 325 of the national sample.

In general, low-income households are less satisfied than higher-income households, are more likely to value transit options and walkability over using a car, and are less confident they will be able to afford a home.

Low-income households are also more likely to live in cities, rural areas, and small towns than in suburbs. Our analysis showed that they are far from a homogeneous group, and there are important differences in the experience of low-income households depending on where they live. For instance, low-income households in cities are more likely to be satisfied with the size and quality of their home than are low-income households in rural areas.

Throughout this report, the results are presented for low-income households separately from households not considered low income in three types of areas: cities, suburbs, and rural areas/small towns. The low-income category comprises all households with incomes below 200 percent of the federal poverty level. Those not considered low income are all households with incomes above 200 percent of the federal poverty level.

In some analyses, data are disaggregated by a more refined set of income categories instead.

$24,000	$39,580
1-person household	3-person household

$32,000	$47,700
2-person household	4-person household

Source: U.S. Department of Health and Human Services.

FIGURE 1

Low-Income Status
All adults, analyzed by major group

	Percentage considered low income
All adults	**29%**
Race/ethnicity	
White	24%
African American	47%
Latino	44%
Generation	
Millennials	41%
Gen Xers	22%
Baby boomers	22%
War/silent	29%
Income	
<$25,000	88%
$25,000–50,000	36%
$50,000–75,000	7%
>$75,000	—
Homeownership	
Own	18%
Rent	47%
Movers	
Very/somewhat likely	34%

Stop me when I come to the category in which your total HOUSEHOLD income fell before taxes last year. Your best estimate is fine. Less than $25,000; $25,000 up to $50,000; $50,000 up to $75,000; $75,000 up to $100,000; $100,000 or more.

Community Types

FIGURE 2

Self-Reported Location
Among all adults

37%
report living
in rural areas or small towns.

26%
report living
in suburbs.

36%
report living
in medium or large cities.

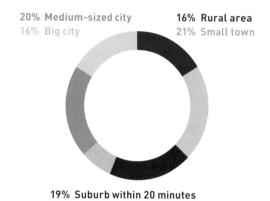

20% Medium-sized city   **16% Rural area**
16% Big city   21% Small town

19% **Suburb within 20 minutes**
7% Suburb farther than 20 minutes

Would you describe where you live as being a rural area, a small town, a
medium-sized city, a big city, a suburb within a 20-minute drive of a city,
a suburb farther than a 20-minute drive to a city, or something else?

Survey respondents were asked to characterize their current residence into one of six location subtypes, ranging from rural area to big city. Responses reflect individuals' opinions about where they live and do not necessarily correspond to places as defined by the U.S. Census Bureau. To simplify findings, for the majority of this report responses are combined into three groups: rural and small-town dwellers, suburbanites, and residents of medium-sized or big cities.

Rural and small-town dwellers. Residents of rural areas and small towns are older, are less culturally diverse, and have a broad range of incomes. Almost half of all members of the war-baby and silent generations—those over age 69—are living in these areas. Rural areas and small-town residents are 78 percent white, 9 percent African American, and 6 percent Latino. Only 26 percent are millennials, while half of these residents are age 50 and older: 32 percent are baby boomers and 18 percent are from the silent/war-baby generations. Thirty-two percent of small-town residents report they are low income.

Suburbanites. Suburban residents are similar in age profile to the residents of small towns and rural areas, but suburbs house a larger share of baby boomers (35 percent are boomers) than any of the other types of areas. Suburbs are 73 percent white, 11 percent African American, and 10 percent Latino. Suburban residents are less likely than rural or city dwellers to be low income, with only 20 percent reporting being in this group.

Residents of big and medium-sized cities. Cities are home to more of the nation's younger generations, composed of 42 percent millennials and 23 percent generation Xers, while only 25 percent of city dwellers are baby boomers and 9 percent are from the silent and war-baby generations. Though predominantly white (59 percent), city residents are the most diverse, with a larger proportion of African American (16 percent) and Latino (17 percent) residents than other areas. Thirty-three percent of city residents are considered low-income.

outdoor recreational spaces, and that traffic and crime make it unsafe to walk in their neighborhoods.

- Despite the fact that fresh, healthy food is a top or high priority for nearly three-quarters of Americans, 16 percent of the country—including 28 percent of African Americans and 25 percent of Latinos—say that healthy food is not easy to find in their communities.

- A quarter of people say that traffic makes it unsafe to walk, and 21 percent say that crime in their neighborhoods makes it unsafe to walk.

- Thirty-eight percent of Americans say there is a lack of convenient outdoor spaces in which to run, walk, or exercise in their community.

WHAT WE WANT
Car Use, Diversity, and Location

When it comes to where they live, Americans are looking for a mix of things. More than half of Americans would like to live in a place where they do not need to use a car very often, and a majority of Americans prefer communities that are diverse.

- Just over half of all Americans (52 percent) and 63 percent of millennials would like to live in a place where they do not need to use a car very often.

- If they could live anywhere, 42 percent of Americans would choose to live in a rural/small-town area, while 37 percent say they live in such a place currently.

- A large majority (78 percent) would rather live in a community where the residents are a mix of ages, and 66 percent would prefer a mix of cultures and backgrounds.

WHERE WE LIVE
Housing Choices and Outlook

Almost half of adults—and three-quarters of millennials—report being somewhat or very likely to move in the next five years. Many millennials report a desire to move out of apartments and into larger spaces and to transition into homeownership while older Americans prefer to stay in their current homes or downsize.

- Forty-eight percent of all Americans and 73 percent of millennials report that they are very or somewhat likely to move in the next five years.

- Seventy-three percent of Americans say that homeownership is a good investment for them, and 72 percent of movers expect to be owners within five years.

- Members of the war-baby/silent generations are more likely than other generations to lack confidence in their ability to afford the home they want in the future, and many expect to downsize their homes or remain in place.

78%
of people would rather live in a community with a mix of ages.

Satisfaction with Communities and Housing

Americans overall express high levels of satisfaction with their communities and the homes in which they live. These expressions of satisfaction are very high for all demographic groups, although they dip among certain groups such as those with lower incomes, millennials, and renters. Low-income people are generally less satisfied than other groups, but their satisfaction can vary by where they live. Overall, people are less satisfied with the range of housing options to choose from in their communities.

87%

of people are satisfied with their community's quality of life.

Satisfaction with Quality of Life in Community

Eighty-seven percent of Americans say they are somewhat or very satisfied with the quality of life in their communities—including nearly half (49 percent) who say they are very satisfied. Satisfaction increases substantially with both age and income. Eighty percent of those earning less than $25,000 per year and 83 percent of millennials are somewhat or very satisfied with their quality of life. This compares with 94 percent of those earning over $75,000 and 92 percent of the war-baby and silent generations.

FIGURE 3

Overall Satisfaction with Communities and Housing
Among all adults

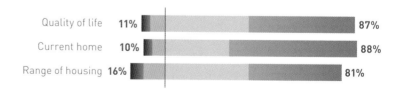

Quality of life	11%	87%
Current home	10%	88%
Range of housing	16%	81%

Very dissatisfied   **Somewhat dissatisfied**   Somewhat satisfied   **Very satisfied**

Now I would like you to tell me how satisfied you are with each of the following: Would you say you are very satisfied, somewhat satisfied, somewhat dissatisfied, or very dissatisfied with [The quality of life in your community.] [The range of different types of housing to choose from in your community.] [The quality and size of the home you live in currently.]

FIGURE 4

Satisfaction with Housing and Community
Among all adults, analyzed by major group

	Quality of life in community		Size and quality of current home		Range of housing in community	
	Total satisfied	Total dissatisfied	Total satisfied	Total dissatisfied	Total satisfied	Total dissatisfied
All adults	**87%**	**11%**	**88%**	**10%**	**81%**	**16%**
Race/ethnicity						
White	88%	9%	88%	9%	81%	14%
African American	84%	16%	88%	12%	79%	19%
Latino	83%	15%	85%	14%	77%	20%
Generation						
Millennials	83%	15%	84%	15%	77%	21%
Gen Xers	87%	11%	88%	11%	80%	17%
Baby boomers	88%	10%	91%	8%	83%	13%
War/silent	92%	5%	93%	3%	87%	6%
Income						
<$25,000	80%	18%	81%	17%	74%	22%
$25,000–50,000	85%	13%	87%	11%	79%	16%
$50,000–75,000	90%	9%	91%	7%	84%	14%
>$75,000	94%	4%	92%	6%	86%	12%
Homeownership						
Own	90%	8%	92%	5%	84%	11%
Rent	82%	18%	80%	19%	73%	25%
Movers						
Very/somewhat likely	82%	17%	82%	17%	74%	23%

Now I would like you to tell me how satisfied you are with each of the following: Would you say you are very satisfied, somewhat satisfied, somewhat dissatisfied, or very dissatisfied with [The quality of life in your community.] [The range of different types of housing to choose from in your community.] [The quality and size of the home you live in currently.]

Low-income Americans are generally less satisfied than those with higher incomes, but their experience is not uniform across different types of communities. Low-income suburbanites are more satisfied than their counterparts in other types of communities. **Low-income people in rural/small-town areas (23 percent) and cities (20 percent) are more likely than low-income suburbanites (8 percent) to register dissatisfaction with their community's quality of life.**

Satisfaction with Current Home

People generally express satisfaction when it comes to where they currently live. Eighty-eight percent of survey respondents overall said they were very or somewhat satisfied with the quality and size of their own home. Eighty-six percent of city dwellers were very or somewhat satisfied, as are 89 percent of suburban and rural/small-town dwellers.

FIGURE 5

Satisfaction with Community Quality of Life
Among all adults, analyzed by income and place

Low income (Household income 200% of federal poverty level and below)		Not low income (Household income above 200% of federal poverty level)
19% ... 78%	Total	8% ... 91%
23% ... 75%	Rural/ small town	6% ... 92%
8% ... 87%	Suburb	5% ... 92%
20% ... 78%	City	11% ... 87%

Very dissatisfied   Somewhat dissatisfied   Somewhat satisfied   **Very satisfied**

Satisfaction with Size and Quality of Current Home
Among all adults, analyzed by income and place

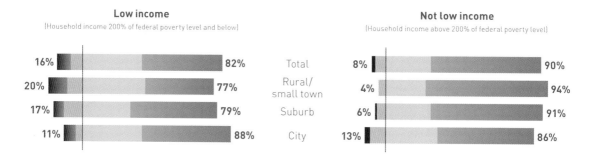

Low income (Household income 200% of federal poverty level and below)		Not low income (Household income above 200% of federal poverty level)
16% ... 82%	Total	8% ... 90%
20% ... 77%	Rural/ small town	4% ... 94%
17% ... 79%	Suburb	6% ... 91%
11% ... 88%	City	13% ... 86%

Very dissatisfied   Somewhat dissatisfied   Somewhat satisfied   **Very satisfied**

Satisfaction with Range of Housing Options from Which to Choose
Among all adults, analyzed by income and place

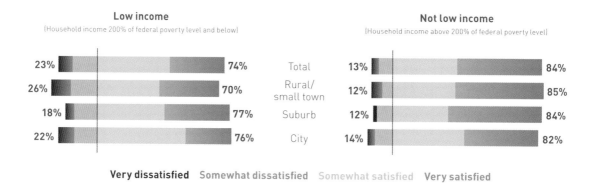

Low income (Household income 200% of federal poverty level and below)		Not low income (Household income above 200% of federal poverty level)
23% ... 74%	Total	13% ... 84%
26% ... 70%	Rural/ small town	12% ... 85%
18% ... 77%	Suburb	12% ... 84%
22% ... 76%	City	14% ... 82%

Very dissatisfied   Somewhat dissatisfied   Somewhat satisfied   **Very satisfied**

Now I would like you to tell me how satisfied you are with each of the following: Would you say you are very satisfied, somewhat satisfied, somewhat dissatisfied, or very dissatisfied with [The quality of life in your community].

Now I would like you to tell me how satisfied you are with each of the following: Would you say you are very satisfied, somewhat satisfied, somewhat dissatisfied, or very dissatisfied with [The quality and size of the home you live in currently].

Now I would like you to tell me how satisfied you are with each of the following: Would you say you are very satisfied, somewhat satisfied, somewhat dissatisfied, or very dissatisfied with [The range of different types of housing to choose from in your community].

93% OF WAR BABIES AND THE SILENT GENERATION ARE SATISFIED WITH THEIR CURRENT HOME.

Eighty-two percent of low-income respondents report being satisfied with their housing, compared with 90 percent of moderate- and higher-income respondents. Eighty-eight percent of low-income city dwellers say they are very or somewhat satisfied, and more than half say they are very satisfied with their current homes. In contrast, low-income rural/small-town residents are the least satisfied with their current homes, with one out of five (20 percent) reporting dissatisfaction with their homes. Rural/small-town areas have a large satisfaction gap between low-income and higher-income residents.

Range of Housing Options

Among the three satisfaction questions, people are least likely to be satisfied with the range of housing to choose from in their community, with 81 percent satisfied and 16 percent dissatisfied. As with the others, satisfaction increases with income and age. However, a number of people in the upper-income bracket—12 percent of those earning more than $75,000—are dissatisfied with the housing options in their community, as are 23 percent of likely movers.

Twenty-six percent of low-income people in rural/small-town areas report being dissatisfied with their community's housing options, and low-income city and suburban residents are close behind with 22 percent and 18 percent dissatisfied, respectively.

WHAT WE VALUE

Community Attribute Priorities

53%

of African Americans say that quality of the environment is a top priority.

The survey asked people about their priorities when it comes to choosing where they live. A healthy environment rises to the top of the priority list, with healthy air and water and access to fresh, healthy food leading the pack. Attributes such as green space, proximity to family and friends, proximity to health care, and walkability are leading priorities for about half the country. Proximity to shopping and entertainment destinations and access to convenient transit are next.

FIGURE 6

Community Attribute Priorities
Percentage of respondents indicating "top" or "high" priority

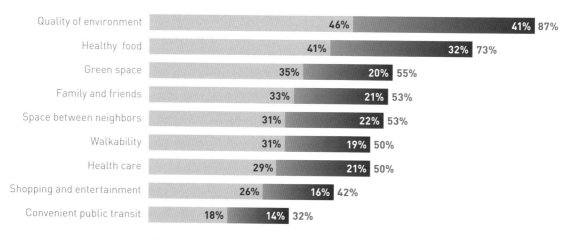

	High priority	Top priority	Total
Quality of environment	46%	41%	87%
Healthy food	41%	32%	73%
Green space	35%	20%	55%
Family and friends	33%	21%	53%
Space between neighbors	31%	22%	53%
Walkability	31%	19%	50%
Health care	29%	21%	50%
Shopping and entertainment	26%	16%	42%
Convenient public transit	18%	14%	32%

High priority   **Top priority**

Let's assume for a minute that you were deciding to stay where you are or to move somewhere else in the next five years. I am going to read some characteristics that you would look for in a neighborhood or community. I would like you to tell me if each would be a top priority, a high but not top priority, a middle priority, or a low priority to you personally in deciding where to live. [How convenient public transportation is.] [How walkable it is, with sidewalks, pedestrian crosswalks, and so forth.] [Whether it's a walk or a short drive to doctors, hospitals, or clinics you use or might need.] [Whether it's a walk or a short drive to shopping and entertainment.] [The availability of fresh, healthy food in the community.] [Having a lot of space between you and your neighbors.] [The quality of the environment, including air and water quality.] [The amount of green space, parks, and recreation areas.] [How close the community is to your family and friends.]

FIGURE 7

Community Attribute Priorities
Percentage of respondents indicating "top" or "high" priority, analyzed by major group

	Quality of environment	Healthy food	Green space	Family and friends	Space between neighbors	Walkability	Health care	Shopping and entertainment	Convenient public transit
All adults	**87%**	**73%**	**55%**	**53%**	**53%**	**50%**	**50%**	**42%**	**32%**
Race/ethnicity									
White	87%	74%	54%	54%	55%	48%	46%	40%	26%
African American	84%	71%	54%	55%	51%	58%	64%	56%	52%
Latino	86%	66%	60%	50%	48%	53%	58%	42%	50%
Generation									
Millennials	87%	71%	56%	50%	50%	54%	50%	44%	39%
Gen Xers	87%	71%	55%	51%	57%	45%	40%	36%	25%
Baby boomers	87%	77%	54%	57%	57%	49%	52%	43%	29%
War/silent	85%	73%	52%	57%	47%	51%	65%	49%	33%
Income									
<$25,000	82%	70%	47%	57%	54%	48%	59%	46%	43%
$25,000–50,000	89%	75%	54%	53%	52%	53%	52%	45%	35%
$50,000–75,000	87%	73%	58%	45%	59%	50%	44%	32%	24%
>$75,000	88%	72%	62%	57%	48%	49%	43%	46%	25%
Homeownership									
Own	88%	73%	56%	56%	55%	46%	47%	39%	25%
Rent	85%	73%	55%	49%	50%	57%	56%	50%	45%
Movers									
Very/somewhat likely	86%	71%	55%	48%	52%	51%	50%	44%	34%

Let's assume for a minute that you were deciding to stay where you are or to move somewhere else in the next five years. I am going to read some characteristics that you would look for in a neighborhood or community. I would like you to tell me if each would be a top priority, a high but not top priority, a middle priority, or a low priority to you personally in deciding where to live. [How convenient public transportation is.] [How walkable it is, with sidewalks, pedestrian crosswalks, and so forth.] [Whether it's a walk or a short drive to doctors, hospitals, or clinics you use or might need.] [Whether it's a walk or a short drive to shopping and entertainment.] [The availability of fresh, healthy food in the community.] [Having a lot of space between you and your neighbors.] [The quality of the environment, including air and water quality.] [The amount of green space, parks, and recreation areas.] [How close the community is to your family and friends.]

Healthy Environment and Food

Environmental quality and the availability of fresh, healthy food emerge as key priorities in the survey.

Americans want to live in communities that provide healthy air and water. **The quality of the environment, including air and water quality, is a top or high priority for 87 percent of Americans** (it is a top priority for 41 percent and high priority for an additional 46 percent). The quality of environment is especially important to African Americans, who rank it a top priority more than any other group (53 percent).

Access to fresh, healthy food was ranked a top (32 percent) or high (41 percent) priority for nearly three-fourths of Americans. African Americans ranked food as a top priority at a higher rate than other Americans—nearly half of this community (47 percent) said that access to healthy food was a top priority. Residents of big cities especially want to live where good food is easily accessible (40 percent top priority).

FIGURE 8

Priority Placed on Availability of Healthy Food and Environmental Quality
Percentage of respondents indicating "top" or "high" priority, analyzed by major group

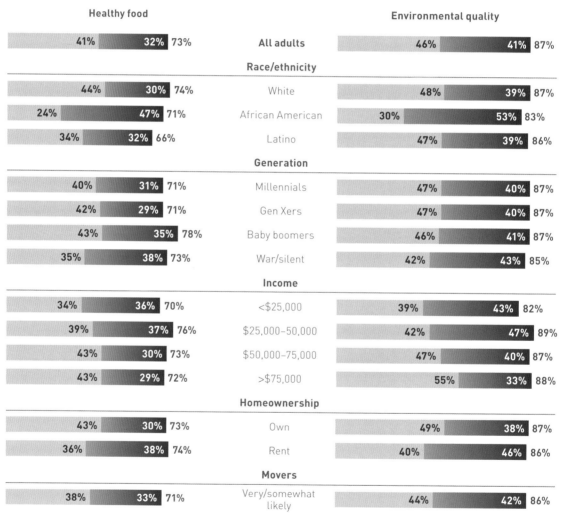

	Healthy food			Environmental quality		
	High	Top	Total	High	Top	Total
All adults	41%	32%	73%	46%	41%	87%
Race/ethnicity						
White	44%	30%	74%	48%	39%	87%
African American	24%	47%	71%	30%	53%	83%
Latino	34%	32%	66%	47%	39%	86%
Generation						
Millennials	40%	31%	71%	47%	40%	87%
Gen Xers	42%	29%	71%	47%	40%	87%
Baby boomers	43%	35%	78%	46%	41%	87%
War/silent	35%	38%	73%	42%	43%	85%
Income						
<$25,000	34%	36%	70%	39%	43%	82%
$25,000–50,000	39%	37%	76%	42%	47%	89%
$50,000–75,000	43%	30%	73%	47%	40%	87%
>$75,000	43%	29%	72%	55%	33%	88%
Homeownership						
Own	43%	30%	73%	49%	38%	87%
Rent	36%	38%	74%	40%	46%	86%
Movers						
Very/somewhat likely	38%	33%	71%	44%	42%	86%

High priority   **Top priority**

Let's assume for a minute that you were deciding to stay where you are or to move somewhere else in the next five years. I am going to read some characteristics that you would look for in a neighborhood or community. I would like you to tell me if each would be a top priority, a high but not top priority, a middle priority, or a low priority to you personally in deciding where to live. [The availability of fresh, healthy food in the community.] [The quality of the environment, including air and water quality.]

FIGURE 9

Priority Placed on Convenient Public Transit
Among all adults, analyzed by income and place

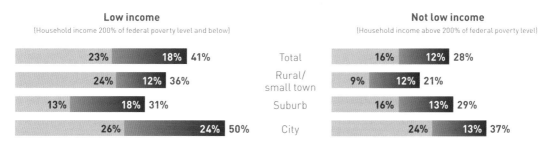

	Low income (Household income 200% of federal poverty level and below)				Not low income (Household income above 200% of federal poverty level)		
Total	23%	18%	41%		16%	12%	28%
Rural/ small town	24%	12%	36%		9%	12%	21%
Suburb	13%	18%	31%		16%	13%	29%
City	26%	24%	50%		24%	13%	37%

High priority   **Top priority**

Let's assume for a minute that you were deciding to stay where you are or to move somewhere else in the next five years. I am going to read some characteristics that you would look for in a neighborhood or community. I would like you to tell me if each would be a top priority, a high but not top priority, a middle priority, or a low priority to you personally in deciding where to live. [How convenient public transportation is.]

Walkability and Transit

Half of Americans prioritize walkable neighborhoods with sidewalks, crosswalks, and other pedestrian-friendly features. Among all Americans, half view walkability as a top or high priority, but when broken down by racial background, it is clear that this feature means more to African Americans (58 percent) than to white Americans (48 percent). Big-city residents (67 percent) are more likely to rate walkability a top or high priority than rural dwellers (32 percent), while those living in small towns (47 percent), suburbs (53 percent), and medium-sized cities (49 percent) fall in between.

The American public is split on how much it values convenient public transportation. A plurality considers convenient public transportation a low priority (44 percent), although a third (32 percent) of people say that convenient public transit in a community is a high (18 percent) or top (14 percent) priority when it comes to where to live. African Americans and Latinos are more likely to highly value access to public transportation than whites.

41% OF LOW-INCOME PEOPLE SAY ACCESS TO PUBLIC TRANSIT IS A TOP OR HIGH PRIORITY.

Low-income people in cities and rural/small towns are more likely than their more affluent neighbors to prioritize public transportation, with half of all low-income residents of cities and 36 percent of rural/small-town residents saying public transit is a top or high priority. However, a sizable portion (37 percent) of those city dwellers who are not low-income also place a high or top priority on public transit when deciding where to live.

BARRIERS TO HEALTHY LIVING

Community Design and Health

38%

of Americans say there is a lack of convenient outdoor spaces in which to run, walk, or exercise in their community.

Despite the high priority placed on healthy community elements, a significant number of Americans face community design–related barriers to living a healthy lifestyle. While the majority of people say they have easy access to fresh food, African Americans and Latinos report greater difficulty. A significant share of the population also says their community lacks outdoor recreational spaces, and that traffic and crime make it unsafe to walk in their neighborhoods. These challenges affect people in all income brackets, although they affect low-income people disproportionately.

FIGURE 10

Assessment of Health-Related Community Characteristics
Percentage of respondents indicating "somewhat" or "strongly" agree

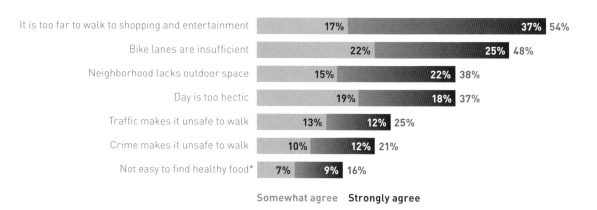

	Somewhat agree	Strongly agree	Total
It is too far to walk to shopping and entertainment	17%	37%	54%
Bike lanes are insufficient	22%	25%	48%
Neighborhood lacks outdoor space	15%	22%	38%
Day is too hectic	19%	18%	37%
Traffic makes it unsafe to walk	13%	12%	25%
Crime makes it unsafe to walk	10%	12%	21%
Not easy to find healthy food*	7%	9%	16%

*Question and responses repositioned to be consistent with other barrier questions.

Please tell me if you agree or disagree with each of these statements: [My neighborhood lacks convenient outdoor spaces to run, walk, or exercise.] [Crime in my neighborhood makes it unsafe to walk.] [Traffic in my neighborhood makes it unsafe to walk.] [We need more bike lanes in my community.] [In the neighborhood where I live, it is too far for people to walk to shopping and entertainment.] [My day is too hectic to accommodate biking and walking.] [It is easy for me to find fresh, healthy food in my community.] Do you [agree/disagree] strongly or somewhat?

FIGURE 11

Assessment of Health-Related Community Characteristics
Percentage of respondents indicating "somewhat" or "strongly" agree, analyzed by major group

	Too far to walk	Need more bike lanes	Lack outdoor space	Day too hectic	Traffic makes unsafe to walk	Crime makes unsafe to walk	Not easy to find fresh food*
All adults	**54%**	**48%**	**38%**	**37%**	**25%**	**21%**	**16%**
Race/ethnicity							
White	58%	44%	33%	33%	21%	17%	12%
African American	51%	55%	49%	50%	35%	35%	28%
Latino	43%	57%	48%	46%	34%	32%	25%
Generation							
Millennials	50%	54%	43%	42%	30%	26%	19%
Gen Xers	53%	48%	35%	41%	22%	17%	15%
Baby boomers	57%	46%	31%	34%	23%	20%	14%
War/silent	61%	36%	42%	32%	23%	19%	12%
Income							
<$25,000	47%	48%	51%	38%	28%	32%	18%
$25,000–50,000	58%	50%	37%	40%	29%	21%	18%
$50,000–75,000	55%	52%	39%	41%	25%	19%	14%
>$75,000	56%	44%	26%	35%	20%	13%	12%
Homeownership							
Own	59%	44%	33%	36%	20%	15%	14%
Rent	47%	54%	45%	40%	33%	33%	19%
Movers							
Very/somewhat likely	52%	53%	40%	40%	29%	25%	19%

*Question and responses repositioned to be consistent with other barrier questions.

Please tell me if you agree or disagree with each of these statements: [My neighborhood lacks convenient outdoor spaces to run, walk, or exercise.] [Crime in my neighborhood makes it unsafe to walk.] [Traffic in my neighborhood makes it unsafe to walk.] [We need more bike lanes in my community.] [In the neighborhood where I live, it is too far for people to walk to shopping and entertainment.] [My day is too hectic to accommodate biking and walking.] [It is easy for me to find fresh, healthy food in my community.] Do you [agree/disagree] strongly or somewhat?

Traffic and Crime as Impediments to Walking

Although most Americans report that it is safe to walk where they live, a significant number of people say their neighborhoods are not safe for pedestrians due to crime or traffic. **One-fifth (21 percent) of Americans say that crime makes it unsafe to walk, and a quarter (25 percent) of people say that traffic makes it unsafe to walk.** Millennials (26 percent), Latinos (32 percent), and African Americans (35 percent) are more likely to say that crime in their neighborhood makes it unsafe to walk. Similarly, millennials (30 percent), Latinos (34 percent), and African Americans (35 percent) are more likely to say that traffic makes it unsafe to walk where they live.

25%

of people say that traffic makes it unsafe to walk in their community.

In all types of communities, low-income residents experience crime at higher rates than people with higher incomes. In cities, 35 percent of low-income residents say that crime makes it unsafe to walk, while 23 percent of people with higher incomes say this is the case where they live. Similarly, a quarter of low-income residents in both suburban and rural/small-town locations say that crime makes walking unsafe, while only 17 percent of suburban and 15 percent of rural/small-town dwellers with higher incomes say they have this problem.

Barriers to Walking and Biking

Despite the desire to be close to amenities, and the fact that walkability is desired by half the country, walking is not a realistic option for many people where they live. More than half of Americans (54 percent) say it is too far

FIGURE 12

Traffic Makes It Unsafe to Walk
Among all adults, analyzed by income and place

Low income
(Household income 200% of federal poverty level and below)

27%	Total	71%
26%	Rural/small town	72%
19%	Suburb	75%
31%	City	68%

Not low income
(Household income above 200% of federal poverty level)

24%	Total	74%
21%	Rural/small town	77%
25%	Suburb	73%
26%	City	72%

Strongly agree Somewhat agree Somewhat disagree **Strongly disagree**

Crime Makes It Unsafe to Walk
Among all adults, analyzed by income and place

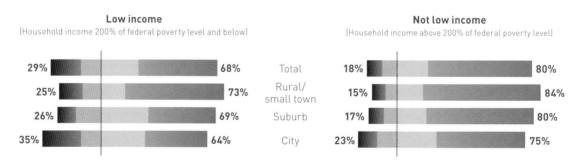

Low income
(Household income 200% of federal poverty level and below)

29%	Total	68%
25%	Rural/small town	73%
26%	Suburb	69%
35%	City	64%

Not low income
(Household income above 200% of federal poverty level)

18%	Total	80%
15%	Rural/small town	84%
17%	Suburb	80%
23%	City	75%

Strongly agree Somewhat agree Somewhat disagree **Strongly disagree**

Please tell me if you agree or disagree with each of these statements: [Traffic in my neighborhood makes it unsafe to walk.] Do you [agree/disagree] strongly or somewhat?

Please tell me if you agree or disagree with each of these statements: [Crime in my neighborhood makes it unsafe to walk.] Do you [agree/disagree] strongly or somewhat?

48% OF PEOPLE BELIEVE THAT THEIR COMMUNITIES NEED MORE BIKE LANES.

to walk to shopping and entertainment in their communities, particularly those in rural areas, where this is true for 80 percent of people.

More than a third of people (37 percent) say that their days are too hectic to accommodate walking and biking. People of color are more likely to feel this way, with half of Latinos (46 percent) and African Americans (50 percent) responding that they do not have time to walk or bike.

Half of all people believe that their communities need more bike lanes. African Americans (55 percent), Latinos (57 percent), and people living in medium-sized cities (56 percent) are slightly more likely to think their communities should have more bike lanes. In cities, low-income people are more likely to strongly agree that their community needs more bike lanes: 35 percent of low-income city dwellers feel this way, while only 21 percent of city dwellers with higher incomes do.

FIGURE 13

It Is Too Far to Walk to Shopping and Entertainment
Among all adults, analyzed by income and place

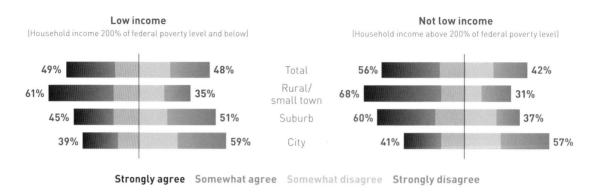

	Low income (Household income 200% of federal poverty level and below)		Not low income (Household income above 200% of federal poverty level)
Total	49% / 48%		56% / 42%
Rural/small town	61% / 35%		68% / 31%
Suburb	45% / 51%		60% / 37%
City	39% / 59%		41% / 57%

Strongly agree   Somewhat agree   Somewhat disagree   **Somewhat disagree**

Please tell me if you agree or disagree with each of these statements: [In the neighborhood where I live, it is too far for people to walk to shopping and entertainment.] Do you [agree/disagree] strongly or somewhat?

Problematic Access to Healthy Food

Most Americans (82 percent) report living in communities where they can easily find fresh food, but 16 percent say they do not. African Americans (28 percent) and Latinos (25 percent) are much more likely than white Americans (12 percent) to say that it is not easy to access fresh, healthy food in their communities.

Low-income Americans are more likely to say that they cannot easily find fresh, healthy food, especially if they live in a rural/small-town area. While 87 percent of higher-income suburbanites can find fresh food easily, only 75 percent of low-income suburbanites say they can. Similarly, while 83 percent of higher-income rural/small-town dwellers say they can find fresh food easily, 73 percent of low-income rural/small-town dwellers say they can. Interestingly, in cities, low-income people and higher-income people appear to have the same access to fresh food—84 percent of both populations say they are able to easily access fresh food.

16% OF THE COUNTRY SAYS THAT HEALTHY FOOD IS NOT EASY TO FIND IN THEIR COMMUNITIES.

Insufficient Outdoor Recreation Space

Over one-third of Americans (38 percent) say that their neighborhood lacks outdoor spaces for exercise, a barrier that varies significantly by demographics and location.

Overall, 51 percent of people with incomes below $25,000 say they do not have access to outside exercise space—twice as many as people with incomes of more than $75,000 per year. In cities, low-income people are significantly more likely than non-low-income people to say their community lacks outdoor space for exercise, while in suburbs and rural/small-town areas the differences are not significant.

Just under half of African Americans (49 percent) and Latinos (48 percent) feel they do not have access to outdoor space for exercise, compared with a third (33 percent) of whites.

FIGURE 14

Neighborhood Lacks Outdoor Space in Which to Exercise
Percentage of respondents indicating "somewhat" or "strongly" agree, analyzed by income

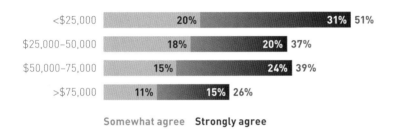

Somewhat agree   **Strongly agree**

Please tell me if you agree or disagree with each of these statements: [My neighborhood lacks convenient outdoor spaces to run, walk, or exercise.] Do you [agree/disagree] strongly or somewhat?

Car Use, Diversity, and Location

When it comes to where we live, Americans are looking for a mix of things. More than half of Americans would like to live in a place where they do not need to use a car very often, a proportion that tracks with the preferences for walkability seen in other sections of this report. Communities that are diverse in age and culture appeal to a majority of Americans. And if they could live anywhere, many Americans would prefer to be in a rural/small-town area.

Location Preferences

Americans live in all types of places, but many say they would like to move somewhere else if they had the option. If they could live anywhere, 42 percent of people say that they would live in a rural/small-town area, compared with 37 percent of people living there today. A plurality of whites (48 percent) are attracted to rural and small-town living, and almost a third (30 percent) of Latinos also show a desire to live in these areas. African Americans, by contrast, show the strongest desire to leave rural areas and cities in order to relocate to the suburbs.

IF THEY COULD LIVE ANYWHERE, **42%** OF AMERICANS WOULD LIVE IN A RURAL/SMALL-TOWN AREA.

The generations also show different desires, which may reflect their different stages of life. Although the city remains the most desirable place for millennials, they show some readiness to relocate to suburbs. Gen Xers and the baby boomers desire rural areas and small towns.

As shown in other sections of this report, despite the pull of rural living, Americans desire proximity to destinations and services. How to meet the combination of demands poses an interesting challenge.

FIGURE 15

Current and Desired Location

Among all adults, analyzed by ethnicity and generation

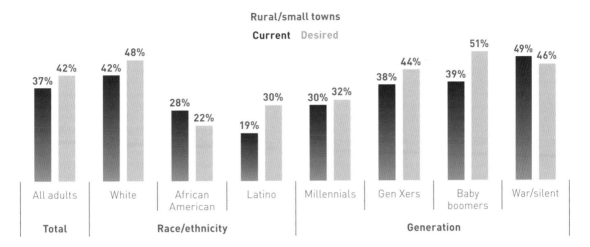

Rural/small towns
Current Desired

	Current	Desired
All adults	37%	42%
White	42%	48%
African American	28%	22%
Latino	19%	30%
Millennials	30%	32%
Gen Xers	38%	44%
Baby boomers	39%	51%
War/silent	49%	46%

Total | **Race/ethnicity** | **Generation**

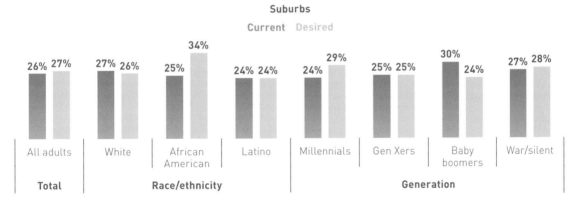

Suburbs
Current Desired

	Current	Desired
All adults	26%	27%
White	27%	26%
African American	25%	34%
Latino	24%	24%
Millennials	24%	29%
Gen Xers	25%	25%
Baby boomers	30%	24%
War/silent	27%	28%

Total | **Race/ethnicity** | **Generation**

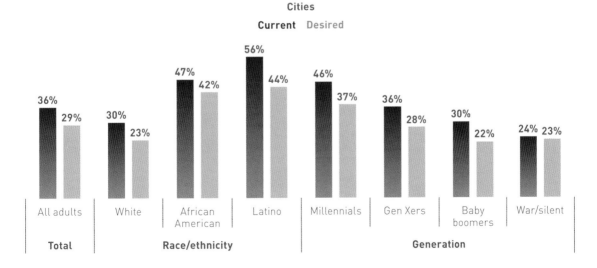

Cities
Current Desired

	Current	Desired
All adults	36%	29%
White	30%	23%
African American	47%	42%
Latino	56%	44%
Millennials	46%	37%
Gen Xers	36%	28%
Baby boomers	30%	22%
War/silent	24%	23%

Total | **Race/ethnicity** | **Generation**

Would you describe where you live as being a rural area, a small town, a medium-sized city, a big city, a suburb within a 20-minute drive of a city, a suburb farther than a 20-minute drive to a city, or something else?

If you could live anyplace in the next five years, would it be a rural area, a small town, a medium-sized city, a suburb within a 20-minute drive of a city, a suburb farther than a 20-minute drive to a city, or something else?

Car-Optional Living

Just over half of Americans (52 percent) agree that they would like to live in a place where they do not need to use a car very often. Less reliance on a car appeals especially to millennials and renters, almost two-thirds of whom (63 percent and 64 percent, respectively) would prefer to live in this kind of "car-optional" place. Approximately 60 percent of the residents of big and medium-sized cities, as well as African Americans and Latinos, are also in favor of car-optional living.

52%
of Americans would like to live in a place where they do not need to use a car very often.

FIGURE 16

Preference for Car-Optional Places
Percentage of respondents indicating "somewhat" or "strongly" agree, analyzed by major group

Group	Somewhat agree	Strongly agree	Total
All adults	24%	27%	52%
Race/ethnicity			
White	24%	25%	49%
African American	21%	38%	59%
Latino	25%	35%	60%
Generation			
Millennials	32%	31%	63%
Gen Xers	22%	23%	44%
Baby boomers	23%	26%	49%
War/silent	15%	27%	42%
Income			
<$25,000	23%	36%	59%
$25,000–50,000	25%	33%	58%
$50,000–75,000	28%	20%	48%
>$75,000	27%	20%	47%
Homeownership			
Own	23%	23%	45%
Rent	28%	36%	64%
Movers			
Very/somewhat likely	28%	31%	59%

Somewhat agree   Strongly agree

Please tell me if you agree or disagree with each of these statements: [I would like to live in a place where I did not need to use a car very often.] Do you [agree/disagree] strongly or somewhat?

FIGURE 17

Preference for Diverse Communities
Percentage of respondents indicating "agree," analyzed by major group

	Variety of ages	Different cultures/ backgrounds
All adults	**78%**	**66%**
Race/ethnicity		
White	80%	61%
African American	69%	81%
Latino	76%	79%
Generation		
Millennials	75%	76%
Gen Xers	82%	72%
Baby boomers	81%	61%
War/silent	73%	44%
Income		
<$25,000	72%	63%
$25,000–50,000	78%	67%
$50,000–75,000	82%	65%
>$75,000	80%	72%
Homeownership		
Own	81%	63%
Rent	74%	71%
Movers		
Very/somewhat likely	76%	69%

[I would rather live in a community where people have a variety of ages] or [I would rather live in a community where most of the people are a similar age].

[I would rather live in a diverse community where people are from different cultures and backgrounds] or [I would rather live in a community where people are mostly from a similar culture and background].

Age and Cultural Diversity

The desire for cultural diversity varies across generations and racial and ethnic groups, but two-thirds of adults (66 percent) prefer to live in communities with a mix of cultures and backgrounds, whereas only half as many (30 percent) say they would prefer living with people who are similar culturally. The desire for cultural diversity declines with each generational cohort.

A large majority of Americans (78 percent) report that they would rather live in a community where the residents are a mix of ages.
This preference is strongest among gen Xers and baby boomers.

❯ WHERE WE LIVE

Housing Choices and Outlook

Almost half of adults—and three-fourths of millennials—report being somewhat or very likely to move in the next five years. Many millennials report a desire move out of apartments and into larger spaces and to transition into homeownership. As baby boomers and older Americans age, they prefer to stay in their current homes or downsize. While most Americans are confident they will be able to afford the home they want, the war-baby/silent generations and low-income people—particularly in suburbs—report that affordability is more of a challenge.

Confidence and Affordability

Most Americans believe they will be able to afford to own or rent the kind of home they want in the next five years, with about 84 percent of the country saying they are somewhat or very confident. Fifty-four percent are very confident and 30 percent are somewhat so, and this confidence is fairly widespread across demographic groups.

However, about 15 percent of the country lacks confidence in their ability to afford the house they want. **Nearly a quarter (22 percent) of the war-baby/silent generations report they are not confident** (15 percent say they are not at all confident, and 7 percent say they are not very confident), a share that is similar to the 25 percent of low-income Americans who lack such confidence.

Moderate- to higher-income residents across all locations maintain similar levels of confidence in their ability to afford the home they want. However, low-income residents in both suburbs and rural/small-town areas report that they are less confident about their ability to afford to own or rent the kind of home they want than are low-income residents of cities. This could be a reflection of overall housing cost differences or other factors such as the lack of availability of stable subsidized or affordable housing in these areas.

FIGURE 18

Confidence in Ability to Afford Desired Home
Among all adults

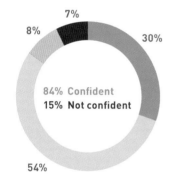

84% Confident
15% Not confident

How confident are you that you will be able to afford to own or rent the kind of home that you want in the next five years? Would you say you are very confident, somewhat confident, not very confident, or not at all confident?

FIGURE 19

Confidence in Ability to Afford Desired Home
Among all adults, analyzed by income and place

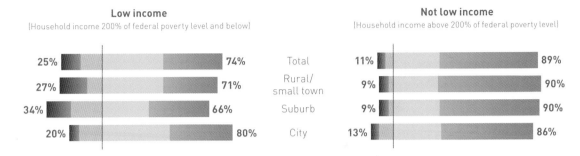

Low income (Household income 200% of federal poverty level and below)		Not low income (Household income above 200% of federal poverty level)	
25% ... 74%	Total	11% ... 89%	
27% ... 71%	Rural/ small town	9% ... 90%	
34% ... 66%	Suburb	9% ... 90%	
20% ... 80%	City	13% ... 86%	

Not at all confident   Not very confident   Somewhat confident   **Very confident**

How confident are you that you will be able to afford to own or rent the kind of home that you want in the next five years? Would you say you are very confident, somewhat confident, not very confident, or not at all confident?

Likely Movers

More Americans report in our 2015 survey that they are very or somewhat likely to move (48 percent) than in our 2013 survey, when 42 percent told us they had plans for a move in the next five years. While the change from 42 percent to 48 percent does not fall outside the margin of sampling error, it could signal a trend to be monitored.

As before, it is the youngest who are the most likely movers. Seven in ten millennials (73 percent) say they are very or somewhat likely to move within five years, compared with just 25 percent of the oldest cohort of the war-baby/silent generations.

Homeownership

Homeownership continues to be a popular goal for Americans—a goal that most are confident they will be able to achieve. **Almost three-fourths (73 percent) say that "buying a home is probably a good investment for me,"** with 25 percent saying that it is probably not so. This figure is virtually unchanged from two years ago, when we last asked this question of the American public.

This optimism is reflected in the finding that 72 percent of those anticipating a move expect to be homeowners in the next five years. The expectation of owning is highest among gen-X movers, and then drops to its lowest point among the war-baby/silent generations. It is also most pronounced among people with the highest incomes, and less certain for those movers in lower economic brackets. African American and Latino homeownership expectations are similar to those of whites, despite large gaps in current homeownership rates.

73%

of millennials report that they are very or somewhat likely to move in the next five years.

72% OF THOSE ANTICIPATING A MOVE EXPECT TO BE HOMEOWNERS IN THE NEXT FIVE YEARS.

Although millennials see themselves transitioning into homeownership as they move into the next phase of their lives, they remain less likely to choose homeownership than gen Xers and the baby boomers in the next five years. In addition, although they are less likely to move, those older Americans in the war-baby and silent generations who are moving expect some degree of transition to rental as they age, with movers in this generation dropping from 77 percent owners to 59 percent owners.

Home Size and Type

Single-family detached homes are the dominant current housing type for Americans as a whole as well as for most demographic groups and generations: 52 percent of millennials report living in single-family detached homes (although 32 percent of this generation say they are still living with parents) and 70 percent or more of all other generations do as well. For low-income households, multifamily housing is more common, with 25 percent of those earning under $25,000 per year and 21 percent of those in the $25,000-to-$50,000 income bracket both living in apartments.

Among likely movers, 41 percent expect their new home to be larger, 23 percent expect it to be smaller, and 35 percent expect it to be the same size. Millennial and gen-X movers are the ones aiming larger (49 and 51 percent, respectively), while 73 percent of baby boomers and 83 percent of the war-baby/silent generations are looking for the same size or smaller quarters.

FIGURE 20

Major Housing Indicators
Among all adults, analyzed by ethnicity and generation

	Somewhat or very likely to move	Very confident in ability to afford desired home	Agree owning a home is a good investment	Current ownership	Expected ownership (among movers)	Looking for larger home (among movers)
All adults	**48%**	**54%**	**73%**	**62%**	**72%**	**41%**
Race/ethnicity						
White	44%	56%	74%	71%	74%	35%
African American	57%	49%	72%	42%	73%	52%
Latino	64%	49%	63%	40%	67%	46%
Generation						
Millennials	73%	52%	74%	37%	69%	49%
Gen Xers	42%	57%	86%	68%	82%	51%
Baby boomers	37%	52%	71%	78%	76%	27%
War/silent	25%	55%	52%	81%	59%	11%
Income						
<$25,000	55%	35%	58%	39%	59%	48%
$25,000–50,000	53%	48%	66%	51%	59%	42%
$50,000–75,000	55%	52%	80%	67%	78%	28%
>$75,000	40%	70%	87%	84%	92%	44%
Homeownership						
Own	34%	59%	77%	100%	82%	29%
Rent	73%	44%	66%	—	64%	51%
Movers						
Very/somewhat likely	100%	50%	76%	44%	72%	41%

How likely are you to move to a different home – one that is your primary residence – in the next five years? Would you say very likely, somewhat likely, not very or not at all likely? How confident are you that you will be able to afford to own or rent the kind of home that you want in the next five years? Would you say you are very confident, somewhat confident, not very or not at all confident? Which of these pairs of statements do you agree with more? [Buying a home is probably a good investment for me] OR [buying a home is probably not so good of an investment for me]. Do you own or rent your primary residence? In five years, do you expect to own or rent your primary residence? Do you expect that when you move, it will be to a smaller home, a larger one, or something about the same size as you have now?

FIGURE 21

Current and Future Housing Type
Among likely movers

	2013		2015	
	Current	Future	Current	Future
Apartment building	26%	15%	24%	13%
Duplex/rowhouse/townhouse	15%	13%	15%	19%
Single-family detached home	56%	67%	55%	61%

Now I have some questions about your home that is your primary residence. Do you currently live in an apartment building; a duplex; a rowhouse or townhouse; a single-family detached home; or something else? How likely are you to move to a different home—one that is your primary residence—in the next five years? Would you say very likely, somewhat likely, not very likely, or not at all likely? In five years, what type of home do you expect to live in? An apartment building; a duplex; a rowhouse or townhouse; a single-family detached house; or something else?

FIGURE 22

Current and Future Housing Types for Millennials
Among millennial likely movers

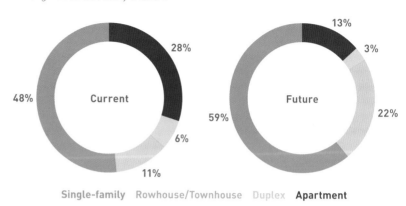

| Single-family | Rowhouse/Townhouse | Duplex | **Apartment** |

Now I have some questions about your home that is your primary residence. Do you currently live in an apartment building; a duplex; a rowhouse or townhouse; a single-family detached home; or something else? How likely are you to move to a different home—one that is your primary residence—in the next five years? Would you say very likely, somewhat likely, not very likely, or not at all likely? In five years, what type of home do you expect to live in? An apartment building; a duplex; a rowhouse or townhouse; a single-family detached house; or something else?

Movers also tend to prefer single-family homes over the other housing types. However, **this year's survey found a somewhat larger share of movers expecting to live in higher-density housing types such as townhomes and duplexes** than in the 2013 results. This year, these housing types represented 19 percent of where likely movers expected to live, up from 13 percent in 2013. In contrast, this year's results showed that 61 percent of movers were expecting to live in single-family detached homes, while our 2013 survey showed that 67 percent of movers would be looking for these kinds of homes. This change in survey responses is something that may signal a shift toward denser living regardless of the location; however, more data will be needed to show that a real shift has occurred.

Millennials represent half of all adults in the survey planning to move in the next five years. Although they do not expect to live in apartments as much as they do currently, twice as many expect to be living in rowhouses or townhouses in the future, and the largest overall share expects to live in single-family homes.